Illustrator

Tony Millionaire

Contributor

Jim Knipfel

Designer

Katya Mezhibovskaya

The DEPRESSION ALPHABET PRIMER

Author

Daniel Riccuito

GINGKO PRESS

The Roaring Twenties came to an abrupt end when the stock market went kablooey in 1929. They were soon replaced by the "Dirty Thirties," a term that, to this day, has come to describe an era in which everything was going to hell—the economy was in ruins, everyone was out of work, crime was rampant, and the general mood of the country could best be described as "utterly, utterly hopeless." America itself seemed to be teetering on the very brink of collapse. But then a big war came along and that made everything better. —Jim Knipfel • • • • • • • •

"AGONY BOX"

Musical slang for a piano

"Get back to beatin' that agony box." - from the film FRISCO JENNY

"ANGEL" *A homosexual*

"ANKLE" *To Walk*

"ACE" *Dollar (Three Card Monte)*

"APSAY" *A sap (Pig Latin)*

"AND HOW!" *Vigorous affirmative*

"ACECRAY OUTCRAY" *Putting the ace on the bottom of the deck, where the dealer can abstract it (Harlem)*

B♭

"BLIND PIG"

Speakeasy

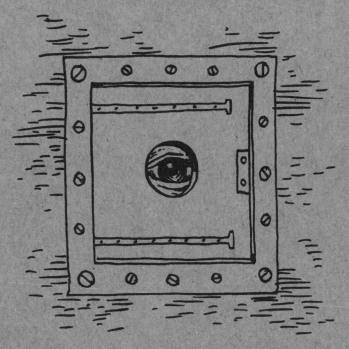

"It beats the devil how a stranger in Chicago can always find a blind pig and get a half-pint for·fifty cents, when the prohibition officials can't locate 'em to save their neck." – from SING SING NIGHTS, a mystery novel by Harry Stephen Keeler

"BROMIDE" *A dull person*

"BEZARK" *A woman or pansy (Underworld)*

"BREEZE" Screw, scram, make an exit (Three Card Monte)

"BERRIES" Money or the wherewithal to play (Three Card Monte)

"BINDLESTIFF"

Homeless wanderer carrying a bundle or "bindle" (Hobo)

"BLANKET" Used in lieu of a table (Three Card Monte)

"CANSKY"

Jail

"The main ghee (guy) is goin' to the cansky in the mornin'."
- from the film BORN RECKLESS

"CASE NOTE" Last dollar (Three Card Monte)

"CAYUSE" Horse

"COO-COO"
Crazy or unconventional

"CHIPPY" Debauched girl (Harlem, also Underworld)

"CINDER DICK" Railroad detective

"CHIVVY" Unpleasant odor (Harlem)

"DICER"

A stiff hat

Other words for hat: skimmer, lid, skull doily . . .

"DRAG" Slow-moving train (Hobo)

"DIZZY-WATER PARLOR" Speakeasy

"DUCAT" Ticket (Carny)

"DINGO" Small-time con man

"DEAFIES"
Panhandlers faking deafness

"DUMMIES"
Panhandlers faking muteness

"D&D'S" *Panhandlers*
faking both deafness and muteness

"EVELYN BRENT"

1930s actress

"I've been so broke a dime would've looked as big as a soup plate."
- from a film called THE SILVER HORDE

"ELBOW-BENDING" Liquor drinking

"EGG" Person, usually male

"EYE ON (SOMEONE), PUT THE" To ogle or leer

"ELEVATE" To rob or "Stick up"

"EGGHEAD" *A bald man*

"EASY MARK" *A person easily victimized (Underworld)*

"FLIRTING WITH THE UNDERTAKER"

To risk one's life

"Tell him that one more crack about me and he's flirting with the undertaker." For such swell threats, see a pip of a "Talkie" from 1932, BLESSED EVENT, starring Mr. Lee Tracy. This film has more snappy one-liners than a Mimi's got screams.

"FIDDLED" Drunk

"FUNNEL" One who drinks intoxicating beverages

"FLIV (OR FLIVVER)" An automobile

"FOLD UP" Be quiet, go away - "Fold up, will ya."

"FITZIES" Panhandlers faking epilepsy

"FIVE HARD" *A fist or a punch (Harlem)*

"FRILL" Girl, woman (Harlem)

"GONIF"

A thief (Yiddish)

In the 1933 Jimmy Cagney film THE PICTURE SNATCHER, Cagney plays a gangster who gets out of prison determined to go straight. His old cronies have different plans, though. They wine and dine him, put him up in swanky hotels, and get him some fancy clothes, all with the idea that he'll pick up where he left off. At the tailor shop, his friends tell the tailor to leave room in his new suit for a gun, but Cagney says no. "Make it fit me," he tells the tailor, who responds in a heavy Yiddish accent, "Don't worry, you'll be the best dressed gonif in America." No, you don't often hear "gonif" — a Yiddish term for "thief" — in everyday conversation anymore, and that's just wrong. — JK

"GOOL" To elicit applause — "My songs will gool 'em in New York."

"GINZO" Any foreigner

"GOBOON" Spittoon

"GAZABO" Guy

"GREASE IT" Pay bribe (Harlem)

"GHEE OR GEE" Guy

H h

"HOOVER DOLLAR"

Empty pocket

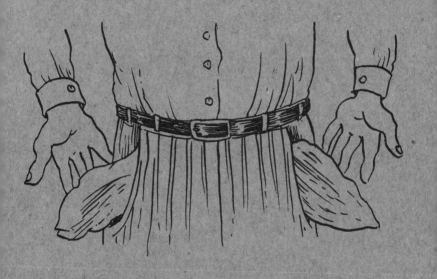

President Herbert H. Hoover was not a very popular man following "Black Tuesday." In fact, his name would become a running joke that betrayed the fury over America's dispossessed and homeless. Old newspapers — slim protection against the elements — were called "Hoover Blankets," empty pockets flapping inside out "Hoover Flags," and shantytowns "Hoovervilles."

"HOPJOINT" Opium den

"HAMBURGER DOWN"
Take it easy (Harlem)

"HOTSPRAT"
Agreeable, light entertainment (Harlem)

"HORSE BLANKET" *A suit*

"HUEY" Nonsense or bull

"HOT SQUAT" Electric chair

"HOCK YOUR SKIN"
Make a difficult promise (Harlem)

"ICEBOX"

Solitary confinement

Also called "the Blue Room" by prisoners.

"ITALIAN-FOOTBALL" Bomb (Detective)

"IGGY" The act of ignoring or feigning ignorance

"IXNAY" A command to stop or "nix" (Pig Latin)

"IN THE HOLE" Out of money (Harlem)

"INK" Cheap wine

"ILLUMINATED" Drunk

"JENNY"

Carny slang for carousel

"Jenny" is slang for an engine, and also means female donkey. Variants include the 'Whirling," "Spinning," or "Flying Jenny" — as well as countless other names for this popular amusement ride.

"JAKE" *Adjective meaning okay, alright, satisfactory*

"JAKE HOUND" *An alcoholic*

"JAZZ-BO" *Fancily dressed person*

"JUNIPER JUICE" Liquor

"JOLT" Prison term

"JOHN" Sucker (Three Card Monte)

"KALE"

Money

Slang words for money (and the lack thereof) teem in the 1930s. Take "skins," meaning dollars in Harlem. Or "skint," which is detective slang for without funds. "Skint" has a close cousin in "skinch," meaning to cheat, and could be a contraction of "skinflint," a miserly person. And yet a simpler guess is that "skint" is a phonetic spelling of "skinned," i.e. in a state of having one's skin(s) removed. These and other colorful expressions, such as "to hock one's skin," reveal how cruel life can be during hard times.

"KICK" *A pocket (Three Card Monte)*

"KIP" *A bed*

"KIBITZ" To offer unwanted advice from "the back seat" as it were, often literally from behind players in a card game (Yiddish)

"KNOCK-OUT-DROPS" Booze

"KAJODY" *A thingamajig*

"KINDERGARTEN" College (Detective)

"LAGERHEAD QUINLAVAN"

Slum kid pal from Cagney's childhood

When he was a lad in the tough Yorkville section of Manhattan, Jimmy Cagney ran with a group of poor slum kids sporting nicknames like "Picky," "Lager-head," and "Specs." One of them, Pete Heslin, was nicknamed "Bootah" on account of the oversized boots he wore. Bootah used to prove how tough he was by hanging off rooftops by his fingertips. Later, he proved how tough he was by becoming a drug addict and killing an off-duty cop during an armed robbery. In 1927 he was sent to Sing Sing and died in the electric chair. Any resemblance between Bootah and Cagney's portrayal of Rocky Sullivan in ANGELS WITH DIRTY FACES is purely intentional. — JK

"LIPPY-CHASER"
A black who prefers whites (Harlem)

"LIT TO THE GUARDS" Intoxicated

"LAY-OUT"
Gambling equipment (Three Card Monte)

"LEATHERED" Unfairly kicked (Harlem)

LAUGHING WATER *Alcohol*

"LAME YOUR FOOT"
Deprive you of assistance (Harlem)

M m

"MAZUMA"

Money

Other words for money: berries, cush, sugar, potatoes, do-re-me . . .

"MUSCLE IN" To use force in a take-over (Underworld)

"MAHOSKA" Illicit drugs

"MAP" A face

"MUZZLER" Obnoxious person (Underworld)

"MUGGLES" Marijuana

"MOB-GHEE" Criminal working with a gang (Underworld)

$N n$

"NECKTIE PARTY"

A hanging

"NOSE CANDY" Cocaine

"NOSE PAINT" Hootch

"NEUTRAL" Adjective describing a stupid or witless person

"NAR" *A fool (Yiddish)*

"NEW FISH"
Newly arrived convict (Prison)

"NINETY-FIVE"
Customer who leaves without paying
(Lunch-counter use)

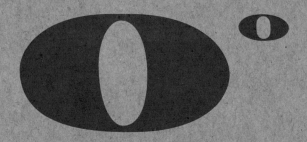

"ON THE BUM"

Broke and homeless

Of course just about anything, from sinks to elbows to luck, can go "on the
bum," a phrase meaning to break down or quit. During the Great Depression,
though, it commonly referred to millions of folks without a fixed address —
like the gentleman pictured above — who might also be called a "bindlestiff"
(see "B" words).

"OWL-EYED" Drunk (Prohibition use)

"ORIE-EYED" Intoxicated

"ODAY" Dough or money (Pig Latin)

"ORANGE" *A baseball*

"OOZE" *To walk sneakily*

"ON THE MUSCLE" *Angry (Detective)*

"PARK THE BODY"

Relax, take a seat

A similar catchphrase of the period reminds us that we're all human. "Be yourself" can convey anything from "relax" to "stop putting on airs" — and even "hey pal, you're nice but not exactly my type." To fend off sweet talk, a woman might say, "Be yourself, I'm dieting." (Check the film CITY STREETS for this and other lost language.)

"PHIZ" Face

"POKEY" A jail

"PUG" A prize fighter

"PAN, ON THE" Being criticized adversely

"PINKTAIL" White person (Harlem)

"PIFFLICATED" Drunk

"QUESTION MARK SHOW"

Carnival attraction

There's no refund. Not on this carnival attraction, which promises nothing and, then, delivers it. A banner reading "?" invites us to step behind the curtain (where we find... three dead shrubs, or a half-eaten sandwich).

"QUEEN" *A ritzy, generous, or attractive woman*

"QUEERIE" *An effeminate man or homosexual*

"QUEER" To spoil or ruin, as in "Shut up mug, you're queering the deal."

"QUEER" Counterfeit money (Three Card Monte)

"QUEER SHOVER"
Fellow who passes counterfeit money (Three Card Monte)

"RUN-OUT POWDER, TAKE A"

To flee

To "take a run-out powder" is to "scram." Or, as film actress Marie Prevost says in THREE WISE GIRLS, "scraminola."

"RAKE-OFF" One's share in the spoils of a criminal enterpri

"RACKET" Any shady business, or swindle

"RUBBERNECK" A prying or gawking person

"RYE-SAP" Rye whiskey (Prohibition use)

"RENO-VATED" Divorced

"RUTABAGA" Homely or ugly woman

"RIGHT GUY" Honest and reliable man

"SOBBY"

A reporter

Also commonly "sob sister" — a purveyor of maudlin stories or simply a journalist.

"SCREWY" Crazy or zany

"SPREADEAGLE" To knock down (Harlem)

"SCRUB THE ONIONS"
A more humble way of saying "tickle the ivories"

"SWACKED OR SWACKO" Drunk

"SLIDE THEM INTO THE CONCRETE"
Eject them into the sidewalk (Harlem)

"SOUP-AND-FISH" A tuxedo

"SCRUB" Face (Harlem)

"SIMOLEON" Dollar (Three Card Monte)

Tt

"TWIST"

A woman

The word "twist" comes from Cockney rhyming slang — "twist and twirl" for girl. Other words denoting the fairer sex include "pancake," "fishcake," "jane," and "frail." My personal favorite is "bezark," taken from underworld lingo and carrying a lightly scornful tone. Film audiences hear James Cagney shout, "Open the gate, bee-zahk!" in 1933, a fateful year that sees spiking unemployment and hunger. In THE MAYOR OF HELL, just as anarchy threatens to spill into the streets, Cagney saves the day (shades of FDR and America's nascent New Deal).

"TRIP HIS MUSCLE" Overreach himself (Harlem)

"THUMB" Use the thumb to displace cards in a poker game (Harlem)

"TIP-OVER" A police raid on a speakeasy

"TOOTSIE ROLL" *A woman*

"TAKE IT [ON THE CHIN]"

To withstand harsh or abusive treatment

"UB IWERKS"

1930s cartoonist

His greatest animated cartoon is BALLOON LAND (1935), also titled THE PIN CUSHION MAN.

"UH-HUH" In love

"UP AGAINST IT" Under enormous pressure, in trouble

"UMBAY" *A bum* (Pig Latin)

"UP AND UP" Honest or fair-minded

"UNGEPOTCH" *Slap-dash, clumsily achieved* (Yiddish)

"UMPCHAY" *A chump* (Pig Latin)

"VARNISH"

Booze

Other words for booze: bellywash, squirrel dew, laughing soup, dream syrup, fun milk, joy juice . . .

"VULCANIZED" Drunk

"VALENTINO" *A handsome man who preys on women*

"VAMP" *To seduce (n. a seductive woman)*

"VEAL CUTLET" Overcoat spread over knees as a playing table (Three Card Monte)

"VESTIBULE" The rump or buttocks

"VELVET" Extra, a perk or luxury

"WHEELER AND WOOLSEY"

1930s comedy duo

See their film CRACKED NUTS!

"WRAPS" Dollars (Harlem)

"WIG" One's head, brain, or mentality

"WHACKS" *A share of the spoils (Detective)*

"WELDED" Married

"WHITE" Good or honest

"WELL OILED" Drunk

"WHOOPIE WATER" Alcohol

"X"

Carny slang for domain

When another vendor has eXclusive rights to ply his trade, you have been "X'd Out."

"XX" Double-cross

"X" Signature of the illiterate

"X JONES OF SCOTLAND YARD"
A 1936 mystery novel by Harry Stephen Keeler

 Cartoon booze

"XLENT" *A '30s brand of salmon*

"YAP"

A gullible or stupid person

Don't confuse this noun for the verb meaning to talk or "gab."

"YIDISHKE" Jewish female (Yiddish)

"YID" Jewish male (Yiddish)

"TO Y" To double-cross (Detective)

"YOU-AND-ME" Tea (Detective)

"YES-GIRL" *A loose young woman*

"YELLOW-BACK"
A banknote or gold certificate

"YENTZ" To cheat (Underworld/Yiddish)

"ZANGARA"

Giuseppe Zangara was
a failed assassin of FDR

Giuseppe Zangara was a short, sickly, poor immigrant who saw capitalists as the root cause of his troubles. In 1933, when newly-elected president Franklin Roosevelt stopped in Miami to give an impromptu speech from the back of his open-topped car, Zangara decided to take care of that part of his problem. Short as he was, he had to stand on a chair to get a clear shot, which made him easy to spot and grab. He still fired five times, missing the President, but hitting four others, killing Chicago Mayor Cermak. He was sent to the electric chair, hating capitalists to the very end. — JK

"ZEKS" Six (Yiddish)

"ZUP" Soup (Yiddish)

"ZOOK" An old prostitute

"ZOWIE" Interjection expressing astonishment

"ZIGZAG" Zigzag (Yiddish)

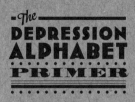

First Published in the United States of America, December 2013.
First Edition.

Gingko Press, Inc.
1321 Fifth Street
Berkeley, CA 94710, USA

www.gingkopress.com

ISBN: 978-1-58423-519-4

© 2013 Text by Daniel Riccuito / Jim Knipfel
© 2013 Illustrations by Tony Millionaire

Printed in China.

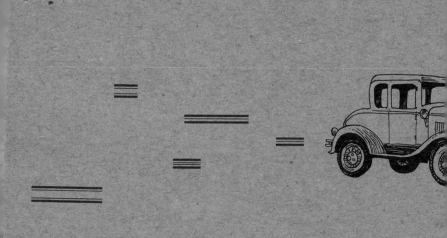